A Numerology Series

by

Lloyd Leon

FOUR

Life Path Four

Contents

Chapter 1

Understanding Life Path 4

The Essence of Life Path 4

The essence of Life Path 4 is deeply rooted in stability, practicality, and a strong sense of responsibility. Individuals on this path are often seen as the builders and organizers of society, possessing a natural inclination to create solid foundations upon which they can construct their lives and the lives of others. This archetype values order and structure, making them reliable friends, partners, and colleagues. Those who resonate with Life Path 4 often find themselves drawn to roles where they can implement systems and processes that foster growth and security.

To truly unlock your potential as a Life Path 4 individual, it is essential to harness your innate ability for time management. The disciplined nature of this life path allows for the establishment of efficient routines that optimize productivity. By creating a structured schedule and prioritizing tasks based on their importance, you can navigate daily challenges with ease. Developing time management strategies that align with your intrinsic need for order can lead to enhanced personal and professional outcomes, ultimately allowing for greater freedom and creativity in other aspects of your life.

Building a strong foundation is a cornerstone of the Life Path 4 experience. Practical skills such as financial literacy, organizational abilities, and project management are vital for those on this journey. Emphasizing the importance of education and continuous learning can significantly impact your ability to create stability. Engaging in workshops, seeking mentorship, or pursuing formal education not only enhances your skill set but also empowers you to take on leadership roles. This proactive approach to personal development fosters a sense of accomplishment and reinforces your role as a dependable figure within your community.

Resilience plays a crucial role in the journey of a Life Path 4 individual. Life is filled with obstacles, and the capacity to overcome challenges is essential for growth. Cultivating resilience techniques such as mindfulness, positive affirmations, and stress management can help you navigate life's ups and downs. Embracing a mindset that views setbacks as opportunities for learning allows you to maintain your focus on long-term goals, reinforcing your commitment to building a secure and fulfilling life. This perseverance not only strengthens your character but also inspires others to adopt a similar outlook.

Creating a balanced life is paramount for individuals on Life Path 4. Striving for harmony between work, relationships, and personal interests ensures that you do not become overwhelmed by responsibilities. Integrating practices such as meditation and self-reflection into your daily routine can aid in maintaining equilibrium. Additionally, fostering nurturing relationships through effective communication and emotional intelligence enhances both personal and professional interactions. By embracing these principles, Life Path 4 individuals can cultivate a fulfilling existence, grounded in the values of stability, practicality, and resilience, while simultaneously unlocking their true potential.

Traits and Characteristics

Individuals on Life Path 4 are characterized by their strong sense of responsibility and commitment to building a secure and stable foundation in their lives. They possess an innate ability to create order from chaos, often gravitating towards structure and organization. This trait makes them exceptional planners and strategists, allowing them to tackle challenges methodically. Life Path 4 seekers are often seen as the pillars of their communities, demonstrating reliability and dependability in all their endeavors. Their grounded nature enables them to remain focused on their goals, often inspiring those around them to adopt a more disciplined approach to life.

Another defining characteristic of Life Path 4 individuals is their practicality. They have a pragmatic mindset that prioritizes functionality and efficiency. This practicality translates into their time management skills, where they excel in creating schedules and sticking to them. Life Path 4 seekers understand the importance of balancing their responsibilities with personal aspirations, enabling them to carve out time for both work and leisure. This characteristic is essential for maintaining harmony in their lives, as it helps them to avoid the pitfalls of overwhelm and burnout.

Life Path 4 individuals are often deeply connected to their values and possess a strong sense of justice. They seek to build a life that reflects their principles, which often leads them to pursue careers that align with their ethical beliefs. This commitment to integrity manifests in their leadership qualities, where they strive to lead by example and inspire others through their actions. Their ability to communicate effectively helps them foster strong relationships, both personally and professionally, allowing them to establish networks that support their ambitions and goals.

Resilience is another hallmark trait of Life Path 4 seekers. When faced with obstacles, they tend to approach challenges with a solutions-focused mindset. This resilience is bolstered by their ability to learn from past experiences, which allows them to adapt and grow. Life Path 4 individuals often view setbacks as opportunities for development rather than failures. This characteristic empowers them to overcome difficulties and persist in their pursuits, reinforcing their foundational belief in hard work and determination.

Lastly, creativity is an essential aspect of Life Path 4 individuals, often manifesting in innovative problem-solving approaches. While they are grounded in practicality, they also appreciate the value of thinking outside the box. This blend of creativity and structure enables them to develop unique solutions that enhance their personal and professional lives. By nurturing their creative side, Life Path 4 seekers can unlock new avenues for growth and fulfillment, ultimately leading to a more balanced and harmonious existence.

The Importance of Structure and Stability

The essence of structure and stability is particularly vital for individuals on the Life Path 4. This life path is characterized by a strong desire for order, practicality, and a solid foundation upon which to build their dreams and aspirations. For Life Path 4 seekers, understanding the significance of creating a reliable framework in their lives can lead to enhanced productivity and a clearer sense of purpose. Structure provides guidance and a roadmap, allowing these individuals to navigate through the complexities of life with confidence, while stability offers the emotional and mental fortitude required to face challenges head-on.

Incorporating effective time management strategies is a crucial aspect of establishing structure for Life Path 4 individuals. By setting specific goals and prioritizing tasks, they can allocate their time efficiently, ensuring that they are focusing on activities that align with their values and long-term objectives. Creating a daily schedule not only helps to enhance productivity but also fosters a sense of accomplishment as tasks are completed. This structured approach to time management can significantly reduce feelings of overwhelm and stress, enabling Life Path 4 seekers to maintain their focus and drive.

Building a strong foundation extends beyond time management; it encompasses the development of practical skills that contribute to overall stability in various aspects of life. Life Path 4 individuals are often called to cultivate skills in organization, planning, and execution. By honing these abilities, they can create a solid base from which to launch their endeavors, whether in personal projects, career aspirations, or relationships. Emphasizing the importance of continuous learning and skill development can empower Life Path 4 seekers to embrace new opportunities and challenges, reinforcing their ability to adapt to changing circumstances while remaining grounded.

Resilience techniques are essential for Life Path 4 individuals as they encounter obstacles on their journey. The stability provided by a strong structure allows them to bounce back from setbacks with greater ease. Techniques such as mindfulness, meditation, and reflective practices enable these individuals to cultivate an inner strength that supports their ability to persevere. By fostering a mindset that embraces challenges as opportunities for growth, Life Path 4 seekers can develop the resilience necessary to navigate life's unpredictability while remaining anchored in their sense of purpose.

Achieving financial stability and planning is another critical component of structure for Life Path 4 individuals. The practical nature of this life path often leads them to prioritize financial security as a means of ensuring a stable environment. By creating a budget, engaging in smart financial planning, and setting realistic savings goals, Life Path 4 seekers can build a strong financial foundation. This financial stability, in turn, enhances their overall sense of security, allowing them to pursue their passions and dreams without the constant burden of financial stress. Through a combination of structured planning and practical skills, Life Path 4 individuals can unlock their true potential and create a balanced life infused with harmony and purpose.

Chapter 2

Unlocking Your True Potential

Identifying Personal Strengths

Identifying personal strengths is a crucial step for those on the Life Path 4 journey. Individuals with this life path are often characterized by their practicality, discipline, and desire for stability. Recognizing and harnessing these inherent strengths can lead to significant personal and professional growth. To begin this process, one must engage in self-reflection and assess personal experiences, skills, and values. This exploration involves looking at past achievements, the activities that bring joy, and the areas where one feels most competent. By understanding what you excel at, you can align your efforts with your true capabilities.

Another effective method for identifying strengths is seeking feedback from others. Friends, family, and colleagues can provide insights that you may not recognize in yourself. They can highlight your unique qualities, such as your ability to organize, your reliability, or your leadership potential. Engaging in conversations about your strengths can also help you gain clarity on how you are perceived in different environments. This external perspective is invaluable, especially for Life Path 4 individuals, who may sometimes be overly critical of themselves and overlook their significant contributions.

Utilizing tools such as personality assessments or strength-finding exercises can further aid in the identification of personal strengths. These tools are designed to uncover innate talents and preferences, providing a structured approach to self-discovery. For Life Path 4 individuals, who often thrive on structure and organization, these assessments can serve as a roadmap for understanding their unique skill set. By analyzing the results, you can pinpoint areas that resonate with your core self, facilitating a deeper connection to your personal and professional aspirations.

Incorporating mindfulness practices can also enhance your ability to identify and appreciate your strengths. Mindfulness encourages present-moment awareness and self-acceptance, allowing you to observe your thoughts and feelings without judgment. This practice can reveal strengths that may have been obscured by doubt or external pressures. For Life Path 4 seekers, dedicating time to meditation or reflective journaling can cultivate an environment where personal strengths can be acknowledged and celebrated, fostering greater confidence and self-assurance.

Finally, aligning your identified strengths with your goals is essential for manifesting your true potential. Once you have a clear understanding of your strengths, you can leverage them in various aspects of your life, including career, relationships, and personal development. Setting specific, actionable goals that tap into these strengths enables you to create a solid foundation for success. For Life Path 4 individuals, this alignment not only enhances productivity but also promotes a sense of fulfillment, as you pursue paths that resonate with your authentic self.

Setting Goals Aligned with Life Path 4

Setting goals that resonate with the essence of Life Path 4 is essential for individuals seeking to unlock their true potential. Life Path 4 embodies the qualities of stability, practicality, and diligence, which means that goal-setting should reflect these attributes. To start, it is crucial to establish clear, attainable objectives that align with your core values and life purpose. This involves a deep self-reflection process where you identify what truly matters to you and how you envision your ideal life. By ensuring your goals resonate with your Life Path 4 characteristics, you will create a strong foundation for personal and professional growth.

Once you have defined your overarching goals, the next step is to break them down into manageable, actionable steps. This aligns with the natural inclination of Life Path 4 individuals to build solid structures. Create a timeline that outlines specific milestones, ensuring each step is realistic and achievable. Incorporating time management strategies, such as prioritizing tasks and setting deadlines, will help you maintain focus and motivation. By treating your goals as a series of smaller objectives, you can reduce overwhelm and track your progress effectively, reinforcing your commitment to achieving them.

In addition to structured goal-setting, it is essential for Life Path 4 individuals to cultivate resilience when facing obstacles. Goals may not always unfold as planned, and setbacks can occur. Developing resilience techniques, such as positive self-talk and problem-solving strategies, will enable you to navigate challenges without losing sight of your objectives. Embrace the idea that obstacles are opportunities for growth, and maintain a flexible mindset that allows you to adjust your goals as needed. This adaptability is vital in fostering a balanced life that harmonizes your ambitions with reality.

Moreover, financial stability plays a significant role in the goal-setting process for Life Path 4 seekers. Setting financial goals that align with your life objectives can create a sense of security and freedom to pursue your passions. Develop a budget and savings plan that supports your aspirations, ensuring you allocate resources effectively. By establishing clear financial goals, you can create a sense of structure that empowers you to take calculated risks in your career and personal life, ultimately leading to greater fulfillment.

Lastly, nurturing relationships and effective communication skills are integral to achieving your goals. As a Life Path 4 individual, fostering connections with like-minded individuals can provide valuable support and encouragement. Surround yourself with a network that shares your values and aspirations, as this community can enhance your motivation and accountability. Additionally, practicing mindfulness and meditation can help you maintain clarity and focus, enabling you to align your daily actions with your long-term goals. By integrating these elements into your goal-setting process, you will cultivate a harmonious and purposeful path that truly reflects the essence of Life Path 4.

Techniques for Self-Discovery

Self-discovery is a profound journey, particularly for those on the Life Path 4. This path emphasizes stability, structure, and practicality, which can sometimes overshadow the need for personal exploration. Engaging in self-discovery techniques allows Life Path 4 individuals to gain clarity about their true selves, aligning their inherent qualities with their goals and aspirations. By embracing various methods, they can cultivate a deeper understanding of their strengths, weaknesses, and potential, ultimately leading to a more fulfilling life.

One effective technique for self-discovery is journaling. This practice encourages Life Path 4 individuals to reflect on their experiences, thoughts, and emotions. By putting pen to paper, they can explore their inner landscapes, identify patterns in their behavior, and articulate their desires. Regular journaling can also help in tracking progress over time, providing insights into personal growth and development. For those who appreciate structure, setting aside a specific time each week for this practice can enhance consistency and deepen the exploration process.

Meditation and mindfulness are also invaluable tools for self-discovery. Life Path 4 individuals can benefit from creating a routine that incorporates these practices, allowing them to center their thoughts and connect with their inner selves. Mindfulness encourages living in the moment, which can reveal insights about personal values and priorities. Simple techniques, such as focusing on breath or engaging in guided meditations, can pave the way for greater self-awareness and emotional regulation. This heightened awareness can inform decision-making and enhance overall well-being.

Engaging in creative activities is another powerful way to unlock self-discovery. Life Path 4 seekers often excel in practical skills, but exploring creativity can lead to new avenues for expression and insight. Whether through art, music, or writing, these pursuits can serve as a means of self-exploration. Creating without judgment allows individuals to tap into their subconscious, uncovering latent talents and passions. Embracing creativity can also foster innovation, ultimately contributing to personal and professional growth.

Lastly, seeking feedback from trusted friends or mentors can offer valuable perspectives in the self-discovery process. Constructive criticism helps Life Path 4 individuals understand how they are perceived by others and can highlight strengths they may not recognize in themselves. By cultivating open and honest communication, they can gain insights that challenge their self-perception and encourage growth. This feedback loop creates an environment for continual learning and adaptation, reinforcing the Life Path 4's foundational goal of building a stable and authentic life.

Chapter 3

Time Management Strategies

Prioritizing Tasks Effectively

Prioritizing tasks effectively is essential for individuals on the Life Path 4 journey, as it enables them to harness their natural strengths and work towards their goals with clarity and purpose. Those with this life path are often characterized by their practicality, reliability, and a strong sense of duty. However, these qualities can sometimes lead to an overwhelming sense of obligation, making it crucial to establish a method for discerning which tasks genuinely deserve attention. By integrating effective prioritization techniques, Life Path 4 individuals can create a structured approach to their daily responsibilities, ensuring they focus on what truly matters.

One effective method for prioritizing tasks is the Eisenhower Matrix, which categorizes tasks into four quadrants based on urgency and importance. Life Path 4 individuals can benefit from this system by assessing their tasks and determining which are both urgent and essential for their long-term goals. By placing emphasis on tasks that align with their core values and aspirations, they can avoid the pitfalls of getting bogged down by less meaningful obligations. This method not only aids in organization but also fosters a sense of empowerment as they take control of their time and energy.

Setting clear goals is another vital aspect of effective task prioritization. Life Path 4 seekers should regularly reflect on their short-term and long-term objectives, aligning their daily tasks with these aspirations. By breaking down larger goals into manageable tasks, they can create a roadmap that guides their actions while maintaining motivation. This process encourages a proactive approach to time management, enabling individuals to track their progress and adjust their priorities as necessary. Through this clarity, they can cultivate resilience, ensuring that setbacks do not derail their overall journey.

Time-blocking is an additional strategy that can significantly enhance task prioritization for Life Path 4 individuals. By allocating specific time slots for different tasks or projects, they can create a structured routine that minimizes distractions and enhances focus. This technique supports their need for stability and organization while allowing for flexibility in the face of unexpected challenges. Life Path 4 individuals can also benefit from setting boundaries around their time, ensuring they dedicate sufficient periods to both work and personal rejuvenation, thus fostering a balanced life.

In conclusion, prioritizing tasks effectively is a transformative practice for Life Path 4 seekers. By employing techniques such as the Eisenhower Matrix, setting clear goals, and utilizing time-blocking, they can navigate their responsibilities with greater ease and intention. This structured approach not only aids in achieving personal and professional objectives but also nurtures their innate qualities of reliability and discipline. Ultimately, mastering the art of prioritization can unlock the true potential of Life Path 4 individuals, enabling them to lead fulfilling lives aligned with their values and aspirations.

Creating a Structured Routine

Creating a structured routine is essential for individuals on Life Path 4, as it provides the foundation necessary for achieving stability and success. Those with this life path are often characterized by their desire for order and practicality. A structured routine not only supports their natural inclinations but also helps them manage their time effectively. By establishing a consistent daily schedule, Life Path 4 seekers can harness their inherent strengths and mitigate the challenges that may arise from a lack of organization.

To begin crafting a structured routine, it is crucial to identify core priorities and values. Life Path 4 individuals thrive when they have clear goals and a sense of direction. This can involve listing personal and professional aspirations, as well as determining the daily activities that align with these targets. By taking the time to reflect on what truly matters, Life Path 4 seekers can create a routine that supports their ambitions and fosters a sense of purpose. This process can also help to eliminate distractions and prioritize tasks that contribute to long-term success.

Once priorities are established, the next step is to design a daily schedule that incorporates these elements. A balanced routine should include time for work, self-care, and personal development. Life Path 4 individuals may benefit from blocking out specific times for tasks such as project work, exercise, and mindfulness practices like meditation. Creating a visual representation of this schedule, whether through a planner or a digital calendar, can enhance commitment and accountability. Additionally, establishing time limits for tasks can help prevent procrastination and encourage a more focused approach to productivity.

Flexibility within a structured routine is equally important. While Life Path 4 individuals often prefer stability, it is essential to allow for adjustments as needed. Life can be unpredictable, and being adaptable ensures that one can respond to unexpected challenges without derailing progress. Incorporating buffer times between tasks can provide the necessary breathing room to accommodate any changes while maintaining the overall structure of the day. This balance between rigidity and flexibility allows for a more resilient approach to daily life.

Ultimately, creating a structured routine enables Life Path 4 individuals to unlock their true potential by fostering a sense of control and purpose. By establishing clear priorities, designing an effective schedule, and allowing for flexibility, they can create a balanced life that nurtures both personal and professional growth. As they cultivate this routine, they will discover that the harmony and structure inherent in their daily lives serve as a catalyst for achieving their dreams and overcoming obstacles with resilience.

Tools and Techniques for Time Management

Time management is an essential skill for individuals on the Life Path 4, who often prioritize stability, organization, and a strong foundation in all aspects of their lives. The right tools and techniques can empower Life Path 4 seekers to navigate their responsibilities effectively while allowing for personal growth and creativity. By mastering time management, they can create a balanced life that honors their commitment to structure and harmony.

One fundamental tool for effective time management is the planner or digital calendar. By scheduling tasks, appointments, and deadlines, Life Path 4 individuals can visualize their commitments and allocate time wisely. A planner not only helps in organizing daily activities but also serves as a reminder of long-term goals. Utilizing color coding or symbols can further enhance clarity, allowing for quick identification of different areas of life such as work, personal development, and relationships.

Another effective technique is the Pomodoro Technique, which encourages focused work sessions followed by short breaks. This method aligns well with the diligent nature of Life Path 4 individuals, allowing them to maintain productivity without overwhelming themselves. By breaking tasks into manageable intervals, they can sustain energy and motivation, making it easier to tackle larger projects without losing sight of their overall objectives.

Prioritization is a critical aspect of time management, particularly for those seeking to build a strong foundation in their lives. The Eisenhower Matrix can be an invaluable tool, helping Life Path 4 seekers distinguish between urgent and important tasks. By categorizing responsibilities, they can focus on what truly matters, ensuring that their energy is directed toward activities that align with their values and long-term aspirations.

Lastly, mindfulness and reflection play a significant role in effective time management. Regularly assessing how time is spent allows Life Path 4 individuals to make necessary adjustments and avoid burnout. Incorporating practices such as journaling or meditation can foster a deeper understanding of personal priorities and enhance overall well-being. By cultivating these skills, Life Path 4 seekers can unlock their true potential, creating a life marked by both achievement and fulfillment.

Chapter 4

Building a Strong Foundation

Essential Practical Skills

Essential practical skills are vital for individuals on the Life Path 4 journey, as they serve as the foundation upon which personal and professional success can be built. Life Path 4 individuals are known for their strong sense of responsibility, practicality, and determination. Cultivating essential skills such as time management, organizational abilities, and financial literacy can significantly enhance their ability to navigate challenges and seize opportunities. Developing these skills will not only empower them to achieve their goals but will also foster a sense of stability and confidence in their endeavors.

Time management is one of the most crucial skills for Life Path 4 seekers. With a natural inclination for structure and order, harnessing effective time management strategies can help them prioritize tasks, set realistic goals, and maintain a healthy work-life balance. Techniques such as the Eisenhower Matrix or time-blocking can be particularly beneficial. By categorizing tasks based on urgency and importance, Life Path 4 individuals can focus their energy on what truly matters, thus reducing stress and enhancing productivity. Regularly reviewing and adjusting their schedules can also ensure that they remain aligned with their long-term objectives.

Organizational skills complement time management and are essential for creating an efficient workflow. Life Path 4 individuals often thrive in environments where systems and processes are in place. Learning to utilize tools such as digital planners, project management software, or simple to-do lists can streamline their daily activities. Developing a habit of decluttering both physical and digital spaces can enhance focus and reduce distractions. By establishing routines and maintaining organization, Life Path 4 seekers can create an environment that supports their ambitions and cultivates a sense of calm amidst the chaos of daily life.

Financial stability is another critical area where practical skills can make a significant difference. Life Path 4 individuals are often practical and grounded, making them well-suited for managing finances effectively. Learning the basics of budgeting, saving, and investing can provide a solid foundation for long-term financial health. Setting clear financial goals and regularly tracking expenses can help them understand their spending habits and identify areas for improvement. Additionally, exploring resources such as financial literacy courses or workshops can enhance their knowledge and empower them to make informed decisions regarding their financial future.

Lastly, developing effective communication skills is essential for nurturing relationships and fostering collaboration. Life

Path 4 individuals are often seen as reliable and trustworthy, qualities that can be enhanced through active listening and empathetic communication. Practicing clear and assertive expression of thoughts and feelings can help them navigate personal and professional relationships more effectively. Engaging in mindfulness practices can also improve self-awareness, enabling them to respond thoughtfully rather than react impulsively in challenging situations. By honing these essential practical skills, Life Path 4 seekers can unlock their true potential and create a life marked by balance, resilience, and purpose.

The Role of Discipline and Organization

Discipline and organization are fundamental pillars for individuals on the Life Path 4 journey. These characteristics serve as the bedrock for achieving stability and success, allowing seekers to align their practical skills with their innate potential. A strong sense of discipline fosters consistency in actions and thoughts, while organization provides the necessary structure to manage various aspects of life effectively. For Life Path 4 individuals, who thrive in environments characterized by order and reliability, cultivating these traits can lead to significant personal and professional growth.

Time management strategies are particularly crucial for Life Path 4 seekers, who often juggle multiple responsibilities. Establishing a routine can help prioritize tasks and allocate time efficiently, ensuring that essential duties are completed while also allowing space for rest and reflection. Utilizing tools like planners or digital calendars can enhance organization, making it easier to visualize commitments. By mastering time management, Life Path 4 individuals can reduce stress and create a balanced life that honors both their ambitions and personal well-being.

Building a strong foundation for Life Path 4 individuals involves not only practical skills but also an understanding of how discipline and organization contribute to overall success. This foundation can include financial stability and planning, which are essential for creating lasting security. By applying disciplined budgeting practices and organized financial tracking, Life Path 4 seekers can cultivate a sense of control over their resources. This stability empowers them to pursue their goals with confidence, knowing they have a solid financial base to support their endeavors.

Overcoming obstacles is another area where discipline and organization play a vital role. Life Path 4 individuals may encounter challenges that test their resilience. By maintaining a disciplined mindset and an organized approach to problem-solving, they can navigate difficulties more effectively. Developing techniques like breaking down larger challenges into manageable steps allows Life Path 4 seekers to maintain focus and motivation, reinforcing their commitment to personal growth and development.

Ultimately, cultivating discipline and organization is essential for Life Path 4 individuals seeking to unlock their true potential. These qualities not only enhance time management and financial planning but also support career development and the nurturing of relationships. By embracing a structured and disciplined approach to life, Life

Path 4 seekers can create harmony and balance, enabling them to thrive in all areas of their journey. This alignment of external organization with internal discipline paves the way for a fulfilling life that resonates with their true purpose.

Creating a Supportive Environment

Creating a supportive environment is essential for individuals on Life Path 4, as it directly impacts their ability to thrive and reach their true potential. Life Path 4 seekers are often characterized by their desire for stability, structure, and practicality. Therefore, cultivating an environment that aligns with these values can significantly enhance their personal and professional growth. This supportive atmosphere should incorporate elements that promote organization, consistency, and a sense of safety, allowing individuals to focus on their goals without unnecessary distractions.

One of the key aspects of creating a supportive environment is establishing a well-organized space. Life Path 4 individuals tend to excel when their surroundings are tidy and structured. This can be achieved through decluttering and arranging personal and workspaces in a way that maximizes efficiency. Consider implementing systems that facilitate easy access to tools and resources, thereby reducing stress and fostering a sense of control. This organized approach not only enhances productivity but also encourages a mindset that values order and routine, which are fundamental for Life Path 4 seekers.

In addition to physical organization, emotional support is equally crucial. Life Path 4 individuals benefit from surrounding themselves with positive influences, including friends, family, and mentors who understand and appreciate their ambitions. Engaging in open communication and sharing goals with these individuals can create a network of encouragement and accountability. This supportive community can help Life Path 4 seekers navigate challenges, celebrate achievements, and maintain motivation. Building relationships based on mutual respect and understanding reinforces the foundation needed for personal growth and resilience.

Moreover, integrating practices that promote mindfulness and self-care into the daily routine can further enhance the supportive environment. Life Path 4 individuals often carry the burden of responsibility, which can lead to stress and burnout. Incorporating mindfulness techniques, such as meditation or journaling, allows for moments of reflection and restoration. These practices help cultivate an inner sense of peace and clarity, enabling Life Path 4 seekers to approach their goals with renewed energy and focus. Creating time for self-care within a structured framework can lead to a more balanced and harmonious existence.

Finally, fostering a culture of learning and development within the supportive environment can significantly benefit Life Path 4 individuals. Encouraging continuous education, whether through formal courses or informal workshops, instills a sense of purpose and growth. This not only enhances practical skills but also cultivates leadership qualities and adaptability, which are vital for navigating life's complexities. A commitment to personal and professional development creates a dynamic environment where Life Path 4 seekers can unlock their true potential and achieve lasting success.

Chapter 5

Overcoming Obstacles

Identifying Common Challenges

Identifying common challenges is crucial for Life Path 4 seekers who strive to unlock their true potential. These individuals often face obstacles that stem from their inherent traits, such as a strong desire for stability and structure. While these qualities can lead to profound achievements, they can also result in rigidity and an aversion to change. Recognizing and addressing these challenges allows Life Path 4 individuals to cultivate resilience and adaptability, essential components for personal growth and success.

One prevalent challenge for Life Path 4 individuals is the tendency to become overwhelmed by their desire for perfection. This drive can hinder their progress, as they may spend excessive time refining their work instead of pursuing new opportunities. The fear of failure often accompanies this perfectionism, leading to procrastination and missed chances for personal and professional development. By acknowledging this pattern, Life Path 4 seekers can implement time management strategies that encourage them to set realistic goals and embrace the concept of progress over perfection.

Another common obstacle is the struggle with rigidity in their routines. Life Path 4 individuals thrive on structure, but an inflexible approach can stifle creativity and hinder growth. This rigidity may manifest as difficulty adapting to new situations or reluctance to explore uncharted territories. To overcome this, practitioners can focus on creating a balanced life that incorporates flexibility within their structured environment. Embracing spontaneity and allowing room for improvisation can lead to enhanced creativity and a broader understanding of their capabilities.

Financial stability poses yet another challenge for those on Life Path 4. While they often exhibit practical skills and a strong work ethic, they may grapple with an overly cautious approach to finances, leading to missed investment opportunities. This mindset can foster anxiety about financial security, which may hinder their ability to take calculated risks. By cultivating a more open-minded perspective towards financial planning and investment strategies, Life Path 4 individuals can pave the way for greater prosperity and abundance.

Lastly, nurturing relationships can be particularly challenging for Life Path 4 seekers, who may prioritize their personal goals over interpersonal connections. This can lead to feelings of isolation and difficulty in communication. Developing effective communication skills and fostering emotional openness are essential for building strong relationships. Engaging in mindfulness and meditation practices can also enhance their emotional intelligence, allowing them to connect more deeply with others while maintaining their foundational stability. By identifying and addressing these common challenges, Life Path 4 individuals can unlock their true potential and lead fulfilling lives.

Resilience Techniques

Resilience is a vital trait for individuals on Life Path 4, who often face obstacles that test their determination and commitment to building a stable and secure life. Understanding and applying resilience techniques can empower Life Path 4 seekers to navigate challenges with grace and emerge stronger. One effective technique is cognitive reframing, which involves altering one's perspective on a situation. By viewing setbacks as opportunities for growth rather than insurmountable barriers, Life Path 4 individuals can maintain motivation and focus on their long-term goals.

Emotional regulation is another crucial resilience technique for Life Path 4 seekers. Developing awareness of one's emotions and learning to manage them effectively can prevent feelings of overwhelm and frustration from derailing progress. Practicing mindfulness and grounding exercises can help in this regard, allowing individuals to remain present and centered during stressful times. By acknowledging emotions without judgment, Life Path 4 individuals can transform negative experiences into valuable lessons, reinforcing their ability to adapt and thrive.

Additionally, establishing a supportive network of relationships is essential for resilience. Life Path 4 seekers should prioritize connections with individuals who uplift and inspire them. Engaging in open and honest communication fosters trust and creates a safe space for sharing challenges and triumphs. This network not only provides emotional support but also offers diverse perspectives and solutions during difficult times. Collaborating with like-minded individuals can lead to innovative ideas and strategies for overcoming obstacles.

Another effective resilience technique involves setting realistic goals and breaking them down into manageable steps. Life Path 4 individuals often possess a strong work ethic, which can lead to overextending themselves. By creating a structured plan that includes achievable milestones, they can stay focused and motivated. Celebrating small victories along the way reinforces a sense of accomplishment and encourages perseverance, making it easier to tackle larger challenges without feeling overwhelmed.

Finally, cultivating a growth mindset is essential for building resilience. Life Path 4 seekers should embrace the idea that challenges and failures are integral parts of the learning process. By viewing themselves as lifelong learners, they can approach obstacles with curiosity rather than fear. This mindset shift allows individuals to persist in the face of adversity, ultimately unlocking their true potential as they navigate their unique life path.

The Power of Perseverance

Perseverance is a fundamental characteristic that can unlock the true potential of individuals on the Life Path 4 journey. It embodies the spirit of determination and resilience, allowing one to navigate the challenges that arise in pursuit of personal and professional goals. For Life Path 4 individuals, who often value structure, stability, and practicality, embracing perseverance can lead to the establishment of a solid foundation for success. By cultivating this quality, you can effectively transform obstacles into stepping stones, enhancing your ability to achieve long-term aspirations and maintain focus on your life's purpose.

In the context of time management, perseverance plays a crucial role. Life Path 4 seekers often find themselves juggling multiple responsibilities, from career goals to personal commitments. Developing the ability to persist through distractions and setbacks can significantly enhance productivity. Establishing a structured routine, setting realistic goals, and maintaining a disciplined approach to time management will enable you to stay committed to your tasks. Each small victory achieved through perseverance reinforces your capacity to manage time effectively, ultimately leading to a more balanced and fulfilling life.

Building a strong foundation requires not only practical skills but also the grit to overcome challenges. Life Path 4 individuals may encounter numerous obstacles on their journey, whether in their careers or personal lives. By fostering an attitude of perseverance, you can learn to view these hurdles as opportunities for growth rather than insurmountable barriers. This mindset shift allows you to develop resilience techniques that empower you to keep moving forward, even when the path seems daunting. Embracing this approach not only enhances your skill set but also encourages a deeper understanding of your innate capabilities.

Creating a balanced life hinges on understanding the importance of harmony and structure. Perseverance enables Life Path 4 individuals to maintain focus on their core values while navigating the complexities of life. By committing to your goals and consistently applying effort, you can cultivate an environment where both personal and professional aspirations thrive. This balance is achieved through dedication to mindfulness and meditation practices that promote self-awareness and emotional regulation. By integrating perseverance into these practices, you reinforce your ability to remain centered and grounded, even amidst external pressures.

Financial stability and career development are critical aspects of the Life Path 4 experience. Perseverance serves as a guiding principle in making sound financial decisions and pursuing purposeful work. By cultivating leadership qualities through persistence, you can inspire others while also paving the way for your own success. The journey may be filled with uncertainties, but with a resilient mindset, you can navigate the complexities of financial planning and career advancement. Ultimately, the power of perseverance not only propels you toward personal growth but also fosters nurturing relationships, enhancing communication skills and enriching your overall life experience.

Chapter 6

Creating a Balanced Life

Understanding Harmony and Structure

Understanding harmony and structure is essential for Life Path 4 individuals as they navigate their journey toward personal fulfillment and success. This path emphasizes the importance of stability, organization, and security in all aspects of life. By grasping the principles of harmony and structure, Life Path 4 seekers can create a solid foundation that fosters growth and resilience. Such an understanding enables them to align their actions with their values, ensuring that their pursuits are both meaningful and sustainable.

Harmony, in the context of Life Path 4, refers to the balance achieved through the integration of various life elements—emotional, physical, and spiritual. For Life Path 4 individuals, achieving this balance requires a conscious effort to prioritize self-care and personal well-being. Engaging in practices that promote emotional health, such as mindfulness and meditation, can enhance their ability to maintain inner peace. Additionally, cultivating supportive relationships contributes to a harmonious environment, allowing Life Path 4 seekers to thrive in their endeavors.

Structure complements harmony by providing the framework within which Life Path 4 individuals can operate effectively. Establishing routines and systems not only enhances productivity but also instills a sense of control and purpose. Time management strategies become crucial, as they allow Life Path 4 seekers to allocate their resources wisely, ensuring that they meet their responsibilities while leaving room for personal growth. Creating a structured environment can minimize stress and distractions, enabling individuals to focus on their goals.

Moreover, embracing challenges and obstacles is a vital aspect of developing resilience, a key quality for Life Path 4 seekers. Understanding that setbacks are a natural part of the journey fosters a mindset that is adaptable and open to learning. By integrating resilience techniques, such as reframing negative experiences and practicing gratitude, Life Path 4 individuals can maintain their focus on long-term objectives. This adaptability, when combined with a structured approach, paves the way for overcoming difficulties and achieving lasting success.

Ultimately, the interplay of harmony and structure in the lives of Life Path 4 seekers leads to a balanced existence where personal and professional aspirations can coexist. By investing in their well-being, establishing routines, and cultivating resilience, individuals can unlock their true potential. This foundation not only supports their journey but also empowers them to inspire others, creating a ripple effect of positive change. Embracing these principles will allow Life Path 4 seekers to thrive in their unique paths, achieving both stability and fulfillment.

Balancing Work and Personal Life

Balancing work and personal life is a critical endeavor for individuals on the Life Path 4 journey, as it directly influences their ability to unlock true potential. Life Path 4 seekers are often characterized by their strong work ethic, practicality, and desire for stability. However, this dedication can lead to an imbalance if not managed effectively. It is essential for Life Path 4 individuals to recognize that while their ambition drives them, nurturing personal relationships and self-care is equally vital for long-term fulfillment.

To achieve this balance, Life Path 4 individuals can employ time management strategies that prioritize both professional responsibilities and personal activities. Creating a structured daily schedule that allocates specific time blocks for work tasks and personal interests can mitigate the risk of burnout. Utilizing tools such as planners or digital calendars can enhance organization, allowing for the inclusion of personal time amidst work commitments. By consciously setting aside moments for relaxation, hobbies, and social interactions, Life Path 4 seekers can foster a more harmonious existence.

Practical skills play a significant role in establishing balance. Life Path 4 individuals are naturally inclined to build solid foundations, and applying this trait to their personal lives can yield profound results. Skills such as effective communication, boundary-setting, and conflict resolution can enhance relationships with family and friends. By being open about their needs and limitations, Life Path 4 seekers can cultivate deeper connections while ensuring that their personal life does not become overshadowed by work demands.

Resilience techniques are also paramount when navigating the challenges of balancing work and personal life. Life Path 4 individuals may encounter stressors that threaten to disrupt their equilibrium. Developing mindfulness practices, such as meditation or journaling, can provide the necessary space for reflection and emotional processing. These techniques help in acknowledging feelings of overwhelm without judgment, empowering Life Path 4 seekers to recalibrate their focus and reinstate balance as needed.

Lastly, cultivating a mindset of flexibility is crucial for maintaining equilibrium. Life Path 4 individuals may find comfort in routine, yet embracing adaptability can lead to growth and enrichment. Understanding that life will present unexpected challenges allows them to navigate changes more gracefully. By integrating a balance of structure and spontaneity, Life Path 4 seekers can enhance their overall well-being, empowering them to unlock their true potential while enjoying a fulfilling personal life.

Strategies for Stress Management

Stress management is a crucial aspect of personal development for Life Path 4 individuals, who often find themselves striving for stability and order in a chaotic world.

Recognizing the unique challenges that come with this life path, it is essential to adopt effective strategies that align with your individual strengths and values. Life Path 4 seekers can benefit from structured approaches to stress management that not only address stressors but also enhance resilience and personal growth.

One effective strategy for managing stress is the practice of time management. Life Path 4 individuals typically thrive on organization and practicality. By implementing a well-structured schedule, you can allocate time for work, relaxation, and personal pursuits. Utilize tools such as planners or digital calendars to prioritize tasks and set realistic deadlines. This proactive approach reduces overwhelm and creates a sense of control, allowing you to navigate life's demands with greater ease.

Another vital aspect of stress management is establishing a strong foundation through practical skills. Life Path 4 seekers often excel in creating systems that foster stability. Engage in activities that build your skill set, such as learning to budget effectively or developing organizational strategies for your home and workspace. These skills not only alleviate stress but also contribute to a sense of accomplishment and security, reinforcing your ability to manage challenges as they arise.

Mindfulness and meditation practices are also integral to stress management for Life Path 4 individuals. Incorporating regular mindfulness exercises into your routine can significantly enhance your emotional resilience. Techniques such as deep breathing, guided imagery, or focused meditation provide an opportunity to center your thoughts and detach from external pressures. By cultivating a mindful mindset, you can approach challenges with clarity and composure, enabling you to respond rather than react to stressors.

Lastly, nurturing relationships and communication skills plays a vital role in stress management. Life Path 4 individuals may sometimes take on too much responsibility, leading to feelings of isolation. Building a support network through open communication can help alleviate stress. Engage in meaningful conversations with trusted friends or family members, and don't hesitate to seek assistance when needed. By fostering connections and sharing your experiences, you can create a balanced support system that enhances your overall well-being and allows you to thrive despite life's challenges.

Chapter 7

Financial Stability and Planning

Budgeting Basics for Life Path 4

Budgeting is a crucial skill for individuals on Life Path 4, who often seek stability and structure in their lives. As a Life Path 4 seeker, it is essential to recognize that financial management is not merely about keeping track of expenses; it is about creating a solid foundation that supports your long-term goals. The disciplined and practical nature of Life Path 4 individuals aligns well with effective budgeting practices, enabling them to harness their innate strengths to achieve financial stability and security.

To begin budgeting effectively, Life Path 4 individuals should start by assessing their income and expenses. This involves taking a thorough inventory of all sources of income, including salaries, freelance work, or investments. Following this, they should categorize their expenses into fixed and variable costs. Fixed costs, such as rent or mortgage payments, are unavoidable, while variable costs, including entertainment and dining out, can be adjusted. By having a clear picture of their financial landscape, Life Path 4 seekers can identify areas where they can cut back or allocate more funds toward savings and investments.

Creating a budget plan is the next step, and it should reflect the core values and goals of Life Path 4 individuals. A practical approach to budgeting often includes the 50/30/20 rule: 50% of income for needs, 30% for wants, and 20% for savings and debt repayment. However, Life Path 4 seekers might find it beneficial to customize these percentages to fit their unique circumstances and aspirations. For instance, they may prioritize savings or investments in personal development, recognizing that these choices align with their desire for stability and growth.

Monitoring and adjusting the budget is an ongoing process that requires discipline and flexibility. Life Path 4 individuals should regularly review their spending habits and savings goals to ensure they remain aligned with their financial objectives. This practice not only helps in maintaining control over finances but also reinforces the importance of resilience and adaptability, which are key traits of Life Path 4. It is vital to celebrate small victories, such as reaching a savings milestone, as this encourages continued commitment to the budgeting process.

Lastly, budgeting should not be viewed as a constraint but rather as a framework that allows Life Path 4 individuals to thrive. By establishing financial boundaries, they create the space necessary for personal growth, creativity, and purposeful work. This balance enables Life Path 4 seekers to focus on their passions without the burden of financial stress. Embracing budgeting as a tool for empowerment can help them unlock their true potential, leading to a harmonious and fulfilling life in alignment with their intrinsic values.

Investing in Your Future

Investing in your future is a crucial aspect for individuals on the Life Path 4 journey. This path is often characterized by a strong desire for stability, practicality, and a solid foundation in both personal and professional realms. To truly unlock your potential, it is essential to approach your future with a strategic mindset, focusing on financial stability, skill development, and personal growth. By prioritizing these areas, you can create a roadmap that not only supports your aspirations but also aligns with the inherent qualities of a Life Path 4.

Financial planning is a cornerstone of investing in your future. Life Path 4 individuals thrive on security and reliability, making it imperative to establish a sound financial strategy. Start by assessing your current financial situation, setting clear goals, and creating a budget that reflects your values and long-term objectives. Consider diversifying your investments to include both traditional avenues, such as stocks and bonds, and alternative options, like real estate or personal development courses. This diversity will provide a safety net while also expanding your opportunities for growth.

In addition to financial investments, developing practical skills is vital for ensuring a stable future. Life Path 4 seekers often excel in areas that require organization, discipline, and hard work. Identify the skills that are most relevant to your career aspirations and invest time in honing them. This might involve enrolling in workshops, pursuing certifications, or engaging in mentorship programs. Building a robust skill set not only enhances your employability but also fosters a sense of confidence and competence that can propel you forward in your personal and professional life.

Resilience is another key element in the investment of your future. Life Path 4 individuals often face challenges that test their determination and ability to adapt. Cultivating resilience techniques will empower you to navigate obstacles with grace and tenacity. Practices such as mindfulness, meditation, and journaling can help you process setbacks and maintain a positive outlook. By viewing challenges as opportunities for growth, you nurture a mindset that is essential for long-term success and fulfillment.

Lastly, nurturing relationships is an integral part of investing in your future. As a Life Path 4 individual, you may find that your connections with others greatly influence your sense of stability and purpose. Focus on building strong, supportive relationships that encourage mutual growth and understanding. Effective communication skills are essential in fostering these connections, so prioritize active listening and empathy in your interactions. By surrounding yourself with like-minded individuals who share your passions and values, you create a network that not only supports your ambitions but also enriches your journey toward realizing your true potential.

Developing Healthy Financial Habits

Developing healthy financial habits is essential for Life Path 4 individuals who seek stability and structure in their lives. This life path is characterized by a strong desire for security, both emotionally and materially. As such, cultivating a solid financial foundation can serve as a catalyst for unlocking true potential. By focusing on practical financial strategies, Life Path 4 seekers can develop habits that not only foster economic well-being but also enhance overall quality of life.

The first step in developing healthy financial habits is setting clear and achievable financial goals. Life Path 4 individuals are naturally organized and methodical, which provides a great advantage when it comes to goal setting. Establish both short-term and long-term financial objectives, such as saving for an emergency fund or planning for retirement. Writing down these goals can further reinforce commitment and accountability. Regularly reviewing and adjusting these goals keeps them relevant and aligned with personal values, ensuring a focused approach to financial stability.

Budgeting is another critical aspect of building healthy financial habits. Life Path 4 seekers thrive on structure, making budgeting an ideal tool for managing expenses and savings. Create a detailed budget that outlines income and expenditures, categorizing spending into necessary and discretionary expenses. This practice not only highlights areas for potential savings but also promotes mindful consumption. By tracking spending habits, individuals can identify patterns and make informed decisions, ultimately leading to better financial health.

Investing in financial education is a vital component of developing healthy financial habits. Life Path 4 individuals often have a strong desire for knowledge and self-improvement. By seeking out resources such as books, online courses, or workshops focused on personal finance, budgeting, and investment strategies, they can cultivate a deeper understanding of their financial landscape. This knowledge empowers Life Path 4 seekers to make informed decisions, mitigate risks, and seize opportunities that align with their financial goals.

Lastly, developing a mindset of gratitude and abundance can transform one's relationship with money. Life Path 4 individuals may sometimes struggle with feelings of scarcity or fear regarding financial matters. By practicing gratitude for what they have and focusing on abundance, they can shift their perspective. Engaging in mindfulness exercises, such as meditation or journaling, can reinforce this mindset. This shift not only enhances emotional well-being but also attracts positive financial opportunities, fostering a healthier and more balanced approach to financial management.

Chapter 8

Cultivating Leadership Qualities

Understanding Leadership Styles

Understanding leadership styles is crucial for individuals on Life Path 4, as it aligns with their innate qualities of stability, structure, and practicality. Leadership is not a one-size-fits-all approach; rather, it encompasses a variety of styles that can be effectively harnessed to enhance personal and professional growth. Life Path 4 individuals often thrive in environments that require organization and reliability, making it essential to identify which leadership style resonates with them and how it can be utilized to unlock their true potential.

One prominent leadership style that aligns well with Life Path 4 is the transformational leadership style. Transformational leaders inspire and motivate others through their vision and enthusiasm, fostering an environment of trust and collaboration. For Life Path 4 individuals, this style can be particularly effective as it encourages them to leverage their strong work ethic and commitment to building solid foundations. By embracing transformational leadership, they can elevate their influence, empowering those around them while staying true to their structured nature.

Conversely, the transactional leadership style may also appeal to Life Path 4 seekers. This style focuses on clear structures, rewards, and performance metrics, which align well with the systematic approach that Life Path 4 individuals often embody. By utilizing transactional leadership, they can create a productive environment that emphasizes accountability and measurable outcomes. This can lead to enhanced team performance and satisfaction, particularly in roles that require diligence and precision.

Furthermore, servant leadership can provide a powerful framework for Life Path 4 individuals. This style emphasizes the importance of serving others and prioritizing their needs while maintaining a sense of community and collaboration. For those on Life Path 4, adopting a servant leadership approach can create a strong sense of loyalty and commitment among team members. By focusing on the growth and well-being of others, they can cultivate an atmosphere of support, which ultimately leads to mutual success and fulfillment.

In conclusion, understanding the various leadership styles available allows Life Path 4 individuals to identify their strengths and areas for growth. By exploring transformational, transactional, and servant leadership styles, they can tailor their approach to fit their unique personalities and circumstances. As they cultivate their leadership qualities, they not only unlock their true potential but also contribute positively to the lives of those they lead.

Embracing these diverse styles will enable them to navigate their personal and professional journeys with confidence and purpose.

Building Confidence and Authority

Building confidence and authority is essential for those on the Life Path 4 journey, as it fosters the ability to manifest their true potential while navigating the complexities of life. Individuals with this path are often seen as practical, diligent, and grounded, yet they may struggle with self-doubt and the fear of stepping into leadership roles. To build confidence, it is important to recognize and appreciate one's unique strengths and the contributions they bring to the table. Engaging in self-reflection can help Life Path 4 individuals identify their achievements and the skills they possess, reinforcing their sense of self-worth and capability.

Establishing a solid foundation is key for Life Path 4 seekers to develop authority. This involves cultivating practical skills that enhance their professional and personal lives. By focusing on time management strategies, individuals can create a structured approach to their daily activities, thus reducing overwhelm and enabling them to make the most of their time. Mastering these skills not only boosts confidence in personal efficiency but also reinforces their ability to lead and inspire others, as they demonstrate reliability and organization in their endeavors.

Resilience is another crucial aspect of building authority. Life Path 4 individuals may face obstacles that challenge their determination and self-belief. Developing resilience techniques, such as reframing negative experiences and practicing positive affirmations, empowers these individuals to bounce back from setbacks and maintain their focus on long-term goals. This internal strength not only builds confidence but also establishes them as dependable figures within their communities, as they exemplify the tenacity to overcome adversity.

Creating a balanced life is also integral to fostering confidence and authority. Life Path 4 individuals can benefit from mindfulness and meditation practices that help them connect with their inner selves, promoting a sense of calm and clarity. By integrating these practices into their daily routines, they can reduce stress and anxiety, allowing their natural leadership qualities to shine through. A balanced approach to life enables them to be more present and engaged, further solidifying their position as trustworthy leaders in both their personal and professional spheres.

Lastly, nurturing relationships and enhancing communication skills play a vital role in establishing authority. By cultivating meaningful connections and effectively expressing their thoughts and ideas, Life Path 4 individuals can inspire and motivate others. They should strive to be active listeners and empathetic communicators, which will not only help them build strong networks but also reinforce their position as credible authorities. Embracing these interpersonal skills, combined with their inherent practicality and resilience, will empower Life Path 4 seekers to unlock their true potential and lead with confidence.

Inspiring Others Through Action

Inspiring others through action is a powerful principle for individuals on the Life Path 4 journey. As you cultivate your own potential, it becomes essential to recognize that your actions can serve as a beacon for those around you. Life Path 4 seekers are naturally inclined toward stability and structure; therefore, demonstrating integrity and reliability in your actions can encourage others to pursue their own paths with confidence. By embodying the values of commitment and perseverance, you not only enhance your own growth but also inspire others to follow suit.

To inspire effectively, it is important to lead by example. This means being proactive in your pursuits and showing resilience in the face of challenges. Life Path 4 individuals often excel in creating systems and processes that promote efficiency and stability. Share your successes and the methods you employed to overcome obstacles, as these stories can motivate others to adopt similar strategies in their lives. Your personal journey, marked by hard work and dedication, can serve as a testament to the rewards of perseverance and can ignite a spark of ambition in those who look up to you.

Moreover, fostering a sense of community is vital in amplifying your impact. Engage with others who share your values and aspirations, creating an environment where support and encouragement thrive. Whether through workshops, discussion groups, or social media platforms, your ability to connect with like-minded individuals can facilitate collective growth. By sharing your experiences and insights, you can help others recognize their own potential and inspire them to take actionable steps toward their goals. Community-building not only bolsters your own journey but also creates a ripple effect of inspiration.

Additionally, consider incorporating mindfulness and reflection into your actions. Life Path 4 individuals benefit greatly from grounding practices that enhance clarity and focus. When you take the time to reflect on your actions and their impact on others, you cultivate a deeper awareness of how your behavior can inspire change. Mindfulness practices, such as meditation or journaling, can provide the insight needed to align your actions with your core values, reinforcing your ability to inspire those around you. This alignment encourages authenticity, which is a powerful motivator for others.

Finally, recognize that the journey of inspiring others is ongoing. As you continue to learn, grow, and evolve, share your new insights and developments with your community. Embrace the role of a lifelong learner, and encourage others to do the same. By being open about your experiences and the lessons you've learned, you create a culture of continuous improvement and support. This not only enhances your own life path but also nurtures an environment where inspiration can flourish, allowing others to unlock their true potential alongside you.

Chapter 9

Mindfulness and Meditation Practices

The Benefits of Mindfulness for Life Path 4

The practice of mindfulness offers Life Path 4 individuals a powerful toolkit for navigating their unique challenges and aspirations. As those on this path often strive for stability, structure, and practicality, mindfulness can enhance their ability to focus and maintain clarity in their objectives. By cultivating a mindful awareness, Life Path 4 seekers can learn to ground themselves in the present moment, reducing the tendency to become overwhelmed by future uncertainties or past regrets. This presence fosters a deeper connection to their core values and goals, ultimately leading to more intentional decision-making.

Mindfulness also aids Life Path 4 individuals in managing their time effectively, a critical aspect of their journey. The structured nature of this life path can sometimes lead to rigidity or a fear of spontaneity. Mindfulness encourages a flexible mindset, allowing individuals to adapt their plans while remaining aligned with their overarching objectives.

Through techniques such as mindful scheduling and prioritization, Life Path 4 seekers can optimize their time management, ensuring they devote energy to tasks that resonate with their purpose and values.

Moreover, the benefits of mindfulness extend to emotional resilience, equipping Life Path 4 individuals to face obstacles with grace. By practicing mindfulness, they can develop a greater awareness of their thoughts and feelings, enabling them to respond rather than react to stressors. This self-awareness fosters resilience, as they learn to recognize and challenge negative patterns or limiting beliefs that may hinder their progress. Through consistent mindfulness practice, Life Path 4 individuals can build a strong emotional foundation that supports their endeavors.

In the realm of relationships, mindfulness plays a crucial role in enhancing communication skills for Life Path 4 seekers. By being fully present during interactions, they can listen more deeply and respond with empathy, fostering stronger connections with others. Mindfulness cultivates patience and understanding, allowing Life Path 4 individuals to navigate conflicts more effectively. This enriched communication not only strengthens personal relationships but also enhances their leadership qualities, as they learn to inspire and motivate others through mindful engagement.

Lastly, the integration of mindfulness into daily life encourages creativity and innovation, essential components for personal growth among Life Path 4 seekers. By creating mental space through mindfulness practices, individuals can unlock new perspectives and ideas that align with their practical nature. This unique blend of creativity and structure can lead to innovative solutions in their careers and personal projects, fostering a sense of fulfillment and purpose. Embracing mindfulness empowers Life Path 4 individuals to not only build a solid foundation but also to explore the limitless possibilities that arise when they allow themselves to think outside the box.

Meditation Techniques for Focus and Clarity

Meditation is a powerful tool for enhancing focus and clarity, particularly for individuals on the Life Path 4, who often value structure and stability. This subchapter will explore various meditation techniques that align with the principles of Life Path 4, helping you cultivate a more centered and mindful approach to life. By dedicating time to these practices, you can improve your concentration and decision-making abilities, essential qualities for achieving your personal and professional goals.

One effective technique is the breath awareness meditation, which involves focusing solely on your breath. Find a quiet space where you can sit comfortably and close your eyes. Inhale deeply through your nose, allowing your abdomen to rise, and then exhale slowly through your mouth. As you concentrate on your breath, thoughts may arise; acknowledge them without judgment and gently guide your focus back to your breathing. This practice not only calms the mind but also sharpens your ability to concentrate on tasks, a vital skill for Life Path 4 individuals who often juggle multiple responsibilities.

Another technique beneficial for enhancing focus is visualization meditation. This method involves picturing a clear and serene image in your mind, such as a calm lake or a peaceful garden. As you visualize this scene, engage all your senses: imagine the sounds, smells, and textures associated with it. This immersive experience can help you clear mental clutter and channel your energy towards specific goals or projects. For Life Path 4 seekers, using visualization can be a powerful way to manifest your aspirations and maintain clarity in your pursuits.

Body scan meditation is another valuable technique for those on this path. In this practice, you systematically focus on different parts of your body, from your toes to the crown of your head. As you bring awareness to each area, you may notice areas of tension or discomfort. This technique not only promotes relaxation but also enhances your connection to your physical self. For Life Path 4 individuals, who often strive for stability, fostering this mind-body connection can lead to greater clarity in decision-making and enhance your overall well-being.

Finally, integrating mindfulness into your daily activities can significantly improve your focus and clarity. Practice being fully present in whatever task you are engaged in, whether it be work, conversation, or even eating. By consciously directing your attention to the present moment, you can reduce distractions and enhance your effectiveness. For Life Path 4 seekers, this practice can create a solid foundation for personal growth, helping you navigate challenges with resilience and insight. By incorporating these meditation techniques into your routine, you unlock the potential for greater focus and clarity in all aspects of your life.

Incorporating Mindfulness into Daily Life

Incorporating mindfulness into daily life can significantly enhance the experience of individuals on the Life Path 4 journey. As Life Path 4 seekers are often grounded, practical, and focused on building strong foundations, the practice of mindfulness allows them to cultivate a deeper awareness of their thoughts, emotions, and surroundings. By integrating mindfulness into their routines, they can foster greater clarity and resilience, enabling them to navigate life's challenges with a centered and balanced approach.

One effective way to begin incorporating mindfulness is through intentional breathing exercises. Setting aside a few moments each day to focus on the breath can ground Life Path 4 individuals, helping them to center their thoughts and release stress. This simple practice encourages a pause in the midst of busy schedules, allowing for reflection and a clearer perspective on daily tasks. By integrating these breathing moments into their time management strategies, they can enhance productivity while maintaining a sense of calm.

Additionally, a mindful awareness of daily activities can transform mundane tasks into opportunities for presence. Whether it's cooking, cleaning, or even walking, being fully engaged in the moment allows Life Path 4 individuals to appreciate the beauty in routine. This practice not only fosters a sense of gratitude but also strengthens their connection to the present, reducing feelings of overwhelm that may arise from future planning or past regrets. Cultivating this awareness can lead to improved emotional stability and a more harmonious life.

Mindfulness meditation offers another powerful tool for Life Path 4 seekers. Setting aside time for meditation can deepen self-awareness and cultivate a sense of inner peace. By focusing on the present moment without judgment, individuals can gain insights into their thought patterns and emotional responses, which is particularly beneficial for those seeking to overcome obstacles and enhance resilience. Regular meditation practice can also encourage a shift in perspective, helping to reframe challenges as opportunities for growth.

Finally, the incorporation of mindfulness into interpersonal relationships can foster stronger communication and deeper connections. Life Path 4 individuals can practice active listening, being fully present in conversations, and responding with intention. This enhances their ability to nurture relationships, as mindful interactions create an atmosphere of trust and understanding. By applying mindfulness to both their personal and professional lives, Life Path 4 seekers can unlock their true potential, build stronger foundations, and cultivate a balanced, fulfilling existence.

Chapter 10

Career Development and Purposeful Work

Identifying Your Career Path

Identifying your career path as a Life Path 4 individual requires a deep understanding of your innate characteristics and how they align with the opportunities available in the professional world. Life Path 4 individuals are known for their practicality, reliability, and strong work ethic. These traits not only guide choices but also provide a solid foundation for building a meaningful career. To begin this journey, it is essential to engage in self-reflection, examining personal interests, values, and skills. This introspection will enable you to uncover what truly excites you and how you can contribute to the world around you.

Once you have an understanding of your passions and strengths, consider how they intersect with various career fields. Life Path 4 seekers often thrive in structured environments that allow for stability and organization. Professions in fields such as project management, finance, engineering, or administration may resonate strongly.

However, the key is not to restrict yourself to traditional roles. Explore opportunities that allow you to apply your methodical approach to creativity or innovation, such as roles in design, technology, or even entrepreneurship. This dual focus on structure and creativity can lead to fulfilling career choices.

Networking is a crucial component of identifying your career path. Engage with professionals in your areas of interest, seek mentorship, and attend industry events. As a Life Path 4, you may find comfort in structured networking opportunities, such as workshops or seminars, where you can learn while connecting with like-minded individuals. Building relationships within your desired field can provide invaluable insights into potential career paths and help you understand the skills and qualifications necessary for success. Additionally, these connections can open doors to job opportunities that align with your aspirations.

Embracing continuous learning is vital for your career development. As a Life Path 4 individual, you may possess a natural inclination towards acquiring practical skills. Seek out courses, certifications, or training programs that enhance your expertise and expand your professional toolkit. This commitment to lifelong learning not only boosts your resume but also reinforces your adaptability in a rapidly changing job market. By staying informed about industry trends and advancements, you position yourself as a competitive candidate, ready to tackle challenges with confidence.

Finally, remember that identifying your career path is an evolving process. As a Life Path 4, you may encounter obstacles that test your resilience and commitment. Embrace these challenges as opportunities for growth and reassessment. Regularly evaluate your career trajectory, and be open to making adjustments that align with your evolving goals and aspirations. By maintaining a balanced approach that incorporates structure, creativity, and adaptability, you can unlock your true potential and carve out a meaningful career path that resonates with your Life Path 4 essence.

Aligning Work with Personal Values

Aligning work with personal values is a crucial aspect for individuals on Life Path 4, as it creates a foundation for both professional fulfillment and personal satisfaction. Those with this life path often seek stability and structure, which can be seamlessly integrated into their work when it resonates with their core beliefs. To achieve this alignment, it is essential to identify your personal values, as they serve as a compass guiding your decisions and actions. Reflecting on what truly matters to you—whether it be integrity, creativity, community, or sustainability—will help clarify your motives and aspirations in your career.

Once you have a clear understanding of your values, the next step is to analyze your current work situation. Assess whether your job or career aligns with those values. This process requires honesty and introspection. Are you working in an environment that supports your beliefs, or do you find yourself compromising them for the sake of stability or financial gain? Life Path 4 individuals often thrive in roles that allow them to create systems and structures that mirror their values, making it essential to seek out opportunities that foster this alignment.

To facilitate this alignment, consider setting specific goals that reflect your values. For instance, if community and service are central to your beliefs, look for career paths that enable you to contribute positively to society. This might involve transitioning to a nonprofit organization, engaging in social entrepreneurship, or incorporating volunteer work into your professional life. By setting these goals, you create a roadmap that not only enhances your career but also ensures that your work is personally meaningful.

Moreover, aligning work with personal values enhances motivation and productivity. When you engage in work that resonates with your core beliefs, you are more likely to feel passionate and driven. This intrinsic motivation can lead to greater job satisfaction and a sense of purpose, which are vital for individuals on Life Path 4 who often struggle with routine and monotony. Cultivating this passion can also inspire creativity and innovation, allowing you to approach your work with fresh ideas and perspectives.

Lastly, remember that aligning your work with your personal values is an ongoing process. As you grow and evolve, your values may shift, requiring regular reassessment of your career path. Embrace this journey as a means of continuous personal and professional development. Engage in mindfulness practices to stay connected to your values and ensure that your work remains a true reflection of who you are. By prioritizing this alignment, you unlock not only your true potential but also enrich your contributions to the world around you.

Strategies for Career Advancement

To effectively advance in your career as a Life Path 4 individual, it is essential to leverage your innate strengths while strategically addressing areas for growth. Life Path 4 seekers are characterized by their practicality, dependability, and strong organizational skills. Recognizing these traits, you can create a focused career advancement plan. Begin by setting clear, achievable goals that align with your values and long-term aspirations. Utilize your analytical skills to break down these goals into smaller, actionable steps, allowing for steady progress and increased motivation. This structured approach not only enhances your productivity but also reinforces your commitment to personal and professional development.

Networking is a crucial element in career advancement, particularly for Life Path 4 individuals who may prefer to work independently. Building relationships with colleagues and industry professionals can provide valuable insights, mentorship opportunities, and potential collaborations. Attend workshops, seminars, and networking events to connect with like-minded individuals who share your interests and professional goals. Additionally, consider joining professional organizations related to your field. Engaging in these communities can broaden your horizons, expose you to new ideas, and help you cultivate relationships that may open doors to new career opportunities.

Continuous learning is vital for staying relevant in today's fast-paced work environment. As a Life Path 4 individual, you thrive on acquiring practical skills that enhance your expertise. Seek out training programs, online courses, or certifications that align with your career objectives. Emphasizing technical skills, project management, and leadership training can significantly elevate your professional profile. Furthermore, dedicate time to self-reflection to identify areas where you can expand your knowledge. Embracing a growth mindset will empower you to adapt and evolve within your chosen career path, ensuring you remain competitive and valuable.

Resilience is another cornerstone of career advancement, especially in the face of challenges. Life Path 4 individuals must recognize that setbacks are a natural part of any career journey. Developing techniques to overcome obstacles—such as maintaining a positive mindset, practicing mindfulness, and seeking support from your network—will help you navigate difficult situations effectively. Building resilience not only enhances your ability to cope with stress but also positions you as a reliable and steadfast leader in the workplace. Your capacity to remain focused and composed under pressure will inspire confidence in your colleagues and superiors alike.

Finally, strive to create a work-life balance that fosters both personal and professional growth. Life Path 4 individuals often excel when they establish structure and harmony in their lives. Incorporate time management strategies to prioritize tasks, ensuring that you allocate time for both career development and self-care. Engage in activities that nurture your creativity and well-being outside of work, as these pursuits can provide new perspectives and inspiration for your professional life. By maintaining a balanced approach, you will not only advance your career but also unlock your true potential as a Life Path 4 individual, achieving fulfillment in all areas of your life.

Chapter 11

Nurturing Relationships

Effective Communication Skills

Effective communication skills are essential for Life Path 4 individuals as they navigate their journeys toward stability and success. Communication is not merely about exchanging information; it involves expressing thoughts and emotions clearly while also being receptive to the perspectives of others. For Life Path 4 seekers, who often prioritize structure and practicality, mastering communication can enhance both personal and professional relationships. By fostering open dialogue and active listening, Life Path 4 individuals can create a solid foundation for collaboration and mutual understanding.

Active listening is a cornerstone of effective communication. It requires full attention and engagement in conversations, allowing individuals to truly understand the message being conveyed. Life Path 4 seekers can benefit from practicing active listening by minimizing distractions, maintaining eye contact, and providing feedback through nods or verbal affirmations. This approach not only demonstrates respect for the speaker but also encourages a deeper connection. By validating others' feelings and viewpoints, Life Path 4 individuals can build trust and strengthen their relationships, whether in personal or professional contexts.

Clarity in expression is equally important for effective communication. Life Path 4 individuals are often detail-oriented and methodical, which can be advantageous when articulating ideas. However, it is essential to strike a balance between being thorough and being concise. Using straightforward language and avoiding jargon can facilitate better understanding among diverse audiences. Additionally, structuring thoughts logically before speaking or writing can help convey messages more effectively. This clarity not only aids in preventing misunderstandings but also showcases the Life Path 4 individual's capability to convey complex ideas with simplicity.

Non-verbal communication plays a significant role in how messages are received. Body language, facial expressions, and tone of voice can all influence the interpretation of spoken words. Life Path 4 seekers should be mindful of their non-verbal cues, ensuring they align with their verbal messages. For instance, maintaining an open posture and using a warm tone can foster a positive atmosphere, encouraging openness in discussions. Being aware of the non-verbal signals of others is equally important, as it allows for a more empathetic and responsive communication style.

Finally, providing constructive feedback is a vital skill for Life Path 4 individuals. Feedback should be approached as a means of fostering growth rather than criticism. When offering feedback, it is crucial to be specific, focusing on behaviors rather than personal attributes. This approach creates a safe space for dialogue, emphasizing improvement and collaboration. Life Path 4 seekers can enhance their leadership qualities by mastering the art of constructive feedback, ultimately contributing to a harmonious and productive environment. By cultivating these effective communication skills, Life Path 4 individuals can unlock deeper connections and navigate their paths with greater confidence and clarity.

Building Strong Connections

Building strong connections is essential for individuals on the Life Path 4 journey, as they often thrive in environments that foster stability, trust, and collaboration. These connections can serve as a solid foundation, helping Life Path 4 seekers not only to feel secure but also to achieve their broader goals. By nurturing relationships, individuals can create a supportive network that encourages personal and professional growth. This chapter will explore strategies to cultivate meaningful connections that align with the unique qualities of Life Path 4 seekers.

One of the primary strengths of Life Path 4 individuals is their ability to create a structured environment. This tendency can be harnessed to build relationships grounded in reliability and dependability. When engaging with others, it is vital to establish clear communication and set expectations that resonate with both parties. By being transparent about intentions and feelings, Life Path 4 individuals can foster trust, which is the cornerstone of any strong relationship. Regular check-ins and open dialogues not only reinforce connections but also allow for the adjustment of boundaries and expectations as relationships evolve.

In addition to communication, it is important for Life Path 4 seekers to actively engage in their communities. This can be achieved through volunteering, attending workshops, or joining groups that share similar interests and values. Such engagements provide opportunities to meet like-minded individuals, thus expanding one's network. Building connections through shared experiences enhances the sense of belonging, which is crucial for Life Path 4 individuals who may sometimes feel isolated in their quest for stability and structure. These community ties can lead to collaborative projects that align with personal goals, further deepening connections.

Another essential aspect of building strong connections is the practice of empathy and active listening. Life Path 4 seekers often have a pragmatic approach to life, but integrating empathy into their interactions can strengthen relationships significantly. By genuinely understanding and validating the feelings and perspectives of others, Life Path 4 individuals can create a safe space for open communication. This not only enhances existing connections but also attracts new ones, as people are naturally drawn to those who show authentic interest and care.

Lastly, maintaining a healthy balance in relationships is key for Life Path 4 seekers. While it is important to invest time and energy into building connections, it is equally vital to ensure that these relationships do not become burdensome. Establishing boundaries and practicing self-care will help Life Path 4 individuals sustain their energy levels and remain engaged in meaningful ways. By prioritizing both personal and relational health, Life Path 4 seekers can build lasting connections that contribute to their overall sense of fulfillment and purpose in life.

Navigating Conflict and Resolution

Navigating conflict is a crucial skill for Life Path 4 individuals, who are often seen as the builders and stabilizers in their communities. Life Path 4 seekers thrive on structure, routine, and reliability, which means that unexpected disruptions can be particularly challenging. Understanding the nature of conflict and its resolution is essential for maintaining personal and professional harmony. As conflict often arises from differing perspectives, Life Path 4 individuals can benefit from developing a mindset that embraces open communication and active listening, providing a solid foundation for resolution.

The first step in navigating conflict is recognizing that it is a natural part of human interaction. Life Path 4 individuals should embrace the idea that conflict does not necessarily indicate failure or discord; rather, it can be an opportunity for growth and deeper understanding. By acknowledging the emotions involved and taking a proactive approach to address them, Life Path 4s can establish a framework for resolution that prioritizes empathy and collaboration. This can lead to constructive conversations that not only resolve the immediate issue but also strengthen relationships in the long run.

Effective conflict resolution requires clear communication skills, a fundamental area of development for Life Path 4 seekers. Practicing assertiveness while remaining respectful can help facilitate discussions that might otherwise become confrontational. It is essential to articulate one's needs and feelings while also being open to the perspectives of others. Utilizing techniques such as "I" statements can help express personal feelings without assigning blame, creating an environment conducive to resolution. This balanced approach aligns with the Life Path 4 emphasis on stability and fairness, ensuring that all parties feel heard and valued.

In addition to communication skills, cultivating emotional intelligence is paramount for resolving conflicts effectively. Life Path 4 individuals should strive to enhance their awareness of their own emotions as well as those of others. This understanding can help them navigate the complexities of interpersonal dynamics during conflict situations. Practicing mindfulness and self-reflection allows Life Path 4 seekers to approach conflicts with a calm demeanor, reducing the likelihood of escalation and fostering a more productive dialogue. Emotional intelligence not only aids in resolving conflicts but also enhances overall relationships, which are vital for personal and professional success.

Finally, developing a structured approach to conflict resolution can provide Life Path 4 individuals with the tools they need to address disputes efficiently. Implementing a step-by-step process, such as identifying the issue, exploring solutions, and agreeing on a mutual resolution, can demystify conflicts and make them more manageable. By viewing conflict as a manageable aspect of life rather than an insurmountable obstacle, Life Path 4 seekers can unlock their true potential. This proactive stance not only facilitates harmonious relationships but also reinforces the foundational qualities of organization and stability that define Life Path 4 individuals.

Chapter 12

Personal Growth through Creativity and Innovation

Embracing Creativity as a Life Path 4

Embracing creativity as a Life Path 4 individual is essential for unlocking your true potential and achieving personal growth. Life Path 4 is often associated with practicality, structure, and a methodical approach to life. However, integrating creativity into your daily routine can provide a much-needed balance, allowing you to break free from rigid patterns and explore new avenues of expression. By embracing creativity, you open yourself up to innovative solutions, fresh perspectives, and a deeper understanding of your own capabilities.

Incorporating creative practices into your life can significantly enhance your time management strategies. For a Life Path 4 individual, who thrives on organization and routine, it may be beneficial to schedule dedicated time for creative activities. Whether it's engaging in art, writing, or other forms of self-expression, this time can serve as a mental reset, fostering both inspiration and productivity. By finding ways to intertwine creativity with your structured lifestyle, you can create a harmonious balance that enhances your overall effectiveness in both personal and professional realms.

Building a strong foundation in practical skills should not overshadow the importance of creative development. Life Path 4 individuals often excel in areas that require discipline and reliability. However, by diversifying your skill set to include creative pursuits, you can enhance your problem-solving abilities and adapt to challenges more effectively. This dual approach allows you to maintain your sturdy foundation while also exploring the fluidity and spontaneity that creativity brings, ultimately leading to a more rounded and resilient character.

Overcoming obstacles is a natural part of any journey, and for Life Path 4 individuals, resilience techniques can be significantly bolstered by creative outlets. Engaging in artistic endeavors or innovative thinking can serve as a coping mechanism during challenging times. Creativity encourages you to step outside your comfort zone, confront fears, and envision solutions that may not have been apparent through conventional thinking. This process not only builds resilience but also fosters a growth mindset, enabling you to view challenges as opportunities for learning and development.

Finally, nurturing relationships through communication skills can be greatly enhanced by a creative approach. Life Path 4 individuals are typically grounded and practical, but incorporating creative expression into your interactions can lead to more meaningful connections. Whether through storytelling, shared activities, or collaborative projects, creativity can serve as a bridge that fosters understanding and empathy. By embracing creativity in your relationships, you cultivate an environment where open dialogue thrives, and deeper connections are formed, enriching both your personal life and your journey as a Life Path 4 seeker.

Innovation in Daily Life

Innovation in daily life is an essential concept for Life Path 4 individuals, who are known for their practicality, organization, and determination. Embracing innovation does not mean abandoning established routines; rather, it involves enhancing them to foster growth and efficiency. For those on this path, integrating innovative practices into everyday activities can lead to a deeper understanding of their potential and help them navigate life's complexities with greater ease. By adopting a mindset that values creativity and adaptation, Life Path 4 seekers can unlock new ways to achieve their goals and fulfill their life's purpose.

One practical approach to innovation in daily life is the implementation of time management strategies that incorporate technology and modern tools. Life Path 4 individuals often thrive in structured environments, and leveraging digital tools can streamline their routines. Applications designed for task management, calendar organization, and project tracking can provide the structure that Life Path 4 seekers crave while introducing flexibility to accommodate spontaneous opportunities. By harnessing these tools, individuals can optimize their productivity, allowing more time for personal growth and exploration of their creative potential.

Building a strong foundation through practical skills is another avenue where innovation can manifest. Life Path 4 individuals excel when they focus on developing competencies that align with their values and strengths. Engaging in lifelong learning, whether through formal education or self-directed study, can introduce new techniques and methodologies that enhance their existing skill set. This commitment to continuous improvement not only fosters personal growth but also positions Life Path 4 seekers as leaders in their fields, as they embrace new ideas and approaches that set them apart from their peers.

As Life Path 4 individuals encounter obstacles, resilience techniques become crucial for maintaining momentum. Innovation in overcoming challenges can involve rethinking traditional solutions and exploring alternative perspectives. For instance, adopting a growth mindset allows individuals to view setbacks as opportunities for learning rather than failures. By cultivating a flexible approach to problem-solving, Life Path 4 seekers can navigate difficulties with confidence and creativity, ultimately emerging stronger and more equipped to handle future challenges.

Finally, creating a balanced life involves harmonizing structure with innovative practices that promote well-being. Mindfulness and meditation can serve as powerful tools for Life Path 4 individuals, helping them center themselves amid the chaos of daily life. By integrating mindfulness techniques into their routines, they can foster a sense of calm and clarity, which enhances their ability to innovate. This balance not only supports their emotional and mental health but also encourages them to explore new avenues for personal and professional development, allowing them to unlock their true potential in all aspects of life.

Fostering a Creative Mindset

Fostering a creative mindset is essential for Life Path 4 individuals, who often thrive on structure and stability. While this foundation is crucial, embracing creativity can enhance problem-solving skills and ignite passion in daily activities. A creative mindset allows for flexibility, enabling Life Path 4 seekers to navigate challenges with innovation. To foster this mindset, it is important to cultivate an environment that encourages exploration and experimentation. Creating a dedicated space for creative pursuits, whether it be through art, writing, or any other form of expression, can stimulate inspiration and help in breaking away from routine.

Daily routines can sometimes become monotonous, restricting the flow of creativity. To counteract this, Life Path 4 individuals should intentionally incorporate activities that spark joy and curiosity. Engaging in hobbies that are outside of their usual interests can expand perspectives and introduce new ideas. For instance, taking a dance class, exploring nature, or even experimenting with cooking can provide fresh experiences that stimulate creative thinking. By stepping outside their comfort zone, Life Path 4 seekers can discover new talents and interests that contribute to a more vibrant and fulfilling life.

Mindfulness plays a significant role in fostering a creative mindset. Practicing mindfulness helps individuals become more aware of their thoughts and feelings, creating space for inspiration to emerge. Techniques such as meditation, deep breathing, or mindful walking can clear mental clutter, allowing for greater focus on creative endeavors. Life Path 4 individuals can benefit from setting aside time each day to engage in mindfulness practices, as this not only enhances creativity but also promotes emotional resilience. When the mind is calm and centered, new ideas are more likely to flow freely.

Collaboration and connection with others can also enhance creativity. Life Path 4 individuals should seek out opportunities to collaborate with like-minded individuals, as sharing ideas can lead to innovative solutions and inspire new ways of thinking. Participating in workshops, community groups, or online forums can create a supportive network that fosters creativity. Engaging in discussions with others can provide valuable feedback and different perspectives, further enriching the creative process.

Lastly, embracing a mindset of growth and experimentation is key for Life Path 4 seekers. Instead of fearing failure, viewing mistakes as opportunities for learning can significantly enhance creativity. Encouraging a playful approach to challenges allows for trial and error without the pressure of perfection. Life Path 4 individuals should remind themselves that creativity is not a linear process; it thrives on exploration and the willingness to take risks. By nurturing this mindset, they can unlock their true potential and lead more fulfilling lives, integrating creativity into their structured approach to achieving goals.

www.ingramcontent.com/pod-product-compliance
Lightning Source LLC
Chambersburg PA
CBHW071927020426
42331CB00010B/2753